Wha makes your body WORK?

Gill Arbuthnott

ILLUSTRATED BY
Marc Mones

A & C BLACK
AN IMPRINT OF BLOOMSBURY
LONDON · NEW DELHI · NEW YORK · SYDNEY

For Isis and Orla (but maybe not just yet!)

First published 2015 by
A & C Black, an imprint of Bloomsbury Publishing Plc
50 Bedford Square, London, WC1B 3DP

www.bloomsbury.com

Bloomsbury is a registered trademark of Bloomsbury Publishing Plc

ISBN 978-1-4729-0886-5

A CIP catalogue for this book is available from the British Library.

Printed in China by Leo Paper Products, Heshan, Guangdong

1 3 5 7 9 10 8 6 4 2

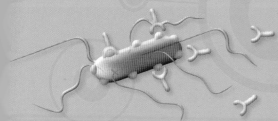
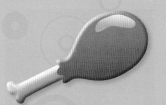

Contents

The Human Body

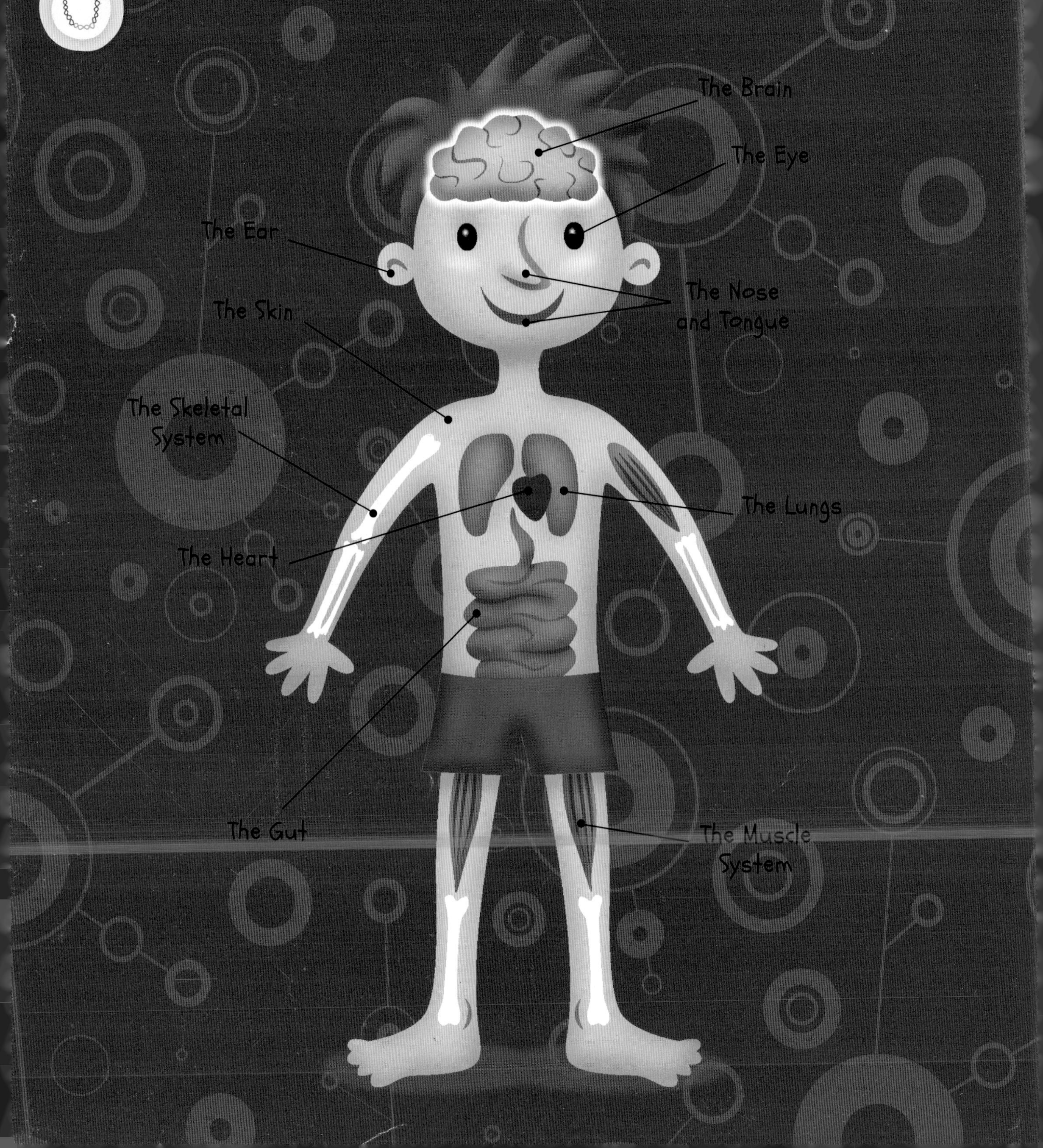

The Brain

The Eye

The Ear

The Nose
and Tongue

The Skin

The Skeletal
System

The Lungs

The Heart

The Gut

The Muscle
System

Introduction

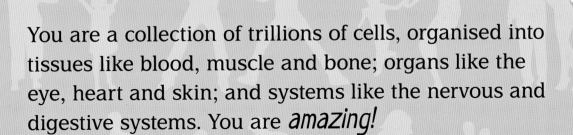

You are a collection of trillions of cells, organised into tissues like blood, muscle and bone; organs like the eye, heart and skin; and systems like the nervous and digestive systems. You are *amazing!*

How do all of these organs work? What can they do? This book takes you on a tour around your own body and shows you how to carry out simple experiments. These experiments will show us just what an incredible living machine the human body is.

Read on and find out...
What makes my
body work?

The Skin

The skin is the largest organ of the body. If you could take it off and spread it out flat it would measure about two square metres. That's about the same area as the mattress of a large single bed.

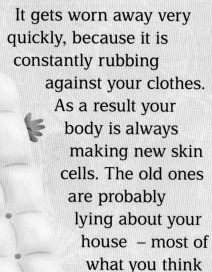

It gets worn away very quickly, because it is constantly rubbing against your clothes. As a result your body is always making new skin cells. The old ones are probably lying about your house – most of what you think is dust is actually dead skin! You lose about a million skin cells every day and replace your entire skin once every four to five weeks, but you don't notice because unlike a snake, you don't do it all at once.

Scars

If your skin is replaced so often, then why don't scars disappear? And what about tattoos – shouldn't they vanish too?

The answer is that the layer of skin that is replaced is the *outer layer*, called the epidermis. Scars are caused by damage to a *deeper layer* of skin called the dermis. This deeper layer of skin isn't replaced in the same way as the outer layer and it's on this deeper layer that tattoo ink sits.

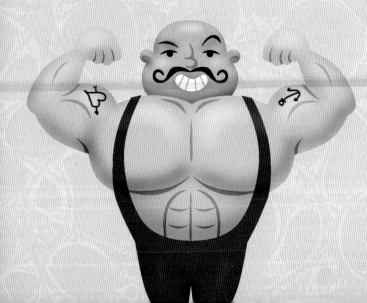

Your skin is essential for a variety of reasons. It's sensitive to touch, pressure, temperature and pain and it is also very important in controlling body temperature. Read on to discover more...

Temperature sensitivity

Your skin is very sensitive to temperature. This doesn't mean that you can put your finger in a glass of water and tell exactly what temperature it is! However, if you dip your finger into two glasses of water, one after another, that are at different temperatures, you can tell which one is warmer – even if the difference is only a few degrees.

TRY IT YOURSELF

1. Ask an adult to help you get two cups of warm water (not too hot – you don't want to burn yourself!) and add a little cold water to one cup. If you have a thermometer, try to get one about five degrees Celsius cooler than the other.

2. Dip your right index finger into the warmer water, and your left index finger into the cooler one.

3. After 30 seconds, swap your fingers to the other cups. You should be able to feel the left finger getting warmer while the right one gets cooler.

Touch

Usually when you want to find out about an object you probably look at it first. But after you've looked at it you might touch it, feel it, or pick it up. We get lots of information about the world around us through our sense of touch, but not all areas of our skin are equally sensitive.

TRY IT YOURSELF

1. Open out a paperclip into a U shape with the two ends about five millimetres apart.

2. Press the points gently against the skin on a fingertip. Can you feel one point or two?

3. Try this on different parts of the body. In some places you will feel two separate points, but in others you will only feel one. This is because some areas have more touch receptors than others.

Control of body temperature

The parts of your skin that help with the control of the body's temperature are the hairs, the sweat glands and the capillaries. If you are cold, the hairs on your body stand on end. Each hair has its own tiny muscle to pull it upright. When the hair does this it traps a layer of warm air next to the skin. In humans this isn't terribly effective, because we're not very hairy, but in other mammals and birds it's very important. This is why small birds and mammals often look 'fluffed up' in cold weather.

When we are cold, blood is also diverted away from the capillaries near the surface of your skin and sent through blood vessels deeper under the skin so it doesn't lose heat. If you are hot, the blood is sent through the skin capillaries so that it can lose heat. Below is an example of a cross section of skin.

The sweat glands in your ears are modified to produce earwax instead of sweat!

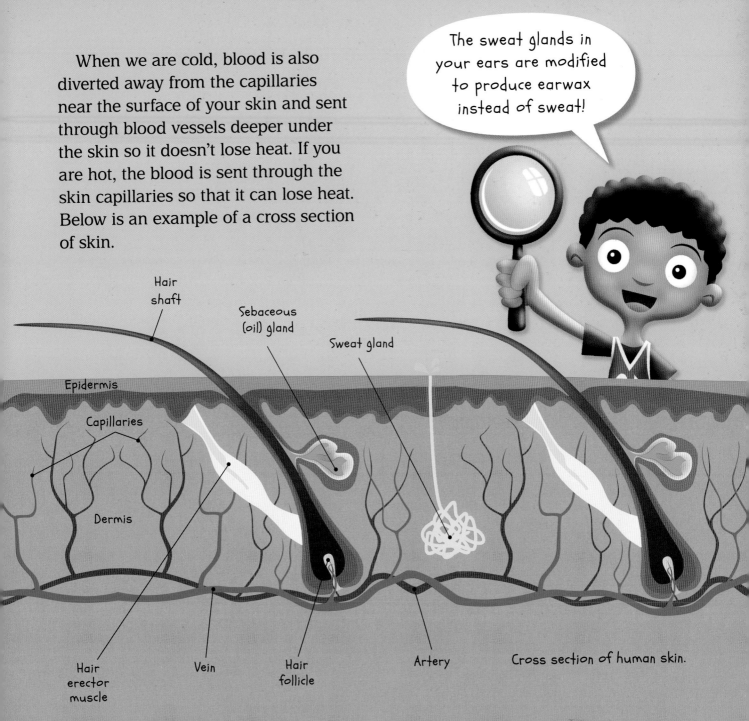

Hair shaft

Sebaceous (oil) gland

Sweat gland

Epidermis

Capillaries

Dermis

Hair erector muscle

Vein

Hair follicle

Artery

Cross section of human skin.

Your sweat glands produce sweat when you are hot, and this is released onto the surface of the skin. As it evaporates, it cools the skin. However this will only work if the sweat does actually evaporate. This works much more efficiently in dry air conditions rather than in humid air, which is why we cope with dry heat better than the humid heat you find in the tropics.

The Heart

Blood is pumped round the entire body by the heart. Your heart acts as a pump in order to do this.

In fact, your heart is really two pumps stuck together side by side. The right side fills with blood from the body and sends it to the lungs to collect oxygen. At the same time the left side fills with the blood from the lungs and sends it to the rest of the body.

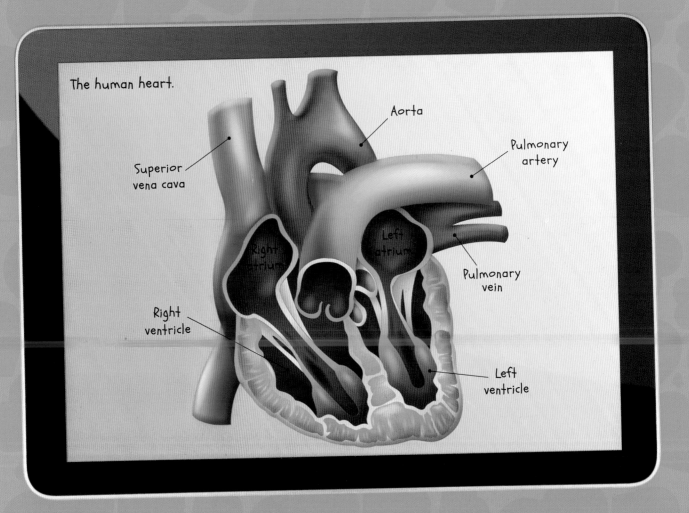

The human heart.

- Superior vena cava
- Aorta
- Pulmonary artery
- Right atrium
- Left atrium
- Pulmonary vein
- Right ventricle
- Left ventricle

Pulse

It's usually quite hard to feel your heart beating, as it's hidden behind your ribs. However, you can feel the squirt of blood pushed out by each heartbeat, which is called the pulse. This happens in places where an artery is near the skin.

Pulse rate varies a lot from person to person, but for an adult, the average is about 70 beats per minute – that's how many times your heart pumps blood each minute.

Your pulse rate varies depending on what you are doing. Take it for a minute when you are sitting doing nothing and make a note of it. Now, if you are fit and healthy, do some exercise; run round the garden, jump up and down, skip, chase the dog – it doesn't matter what it is! Do enough to make you breathe hard.

As soon as you stop, take your pulse again. It will be faster than before. This is because your muscles need extra supplies of blood brought to them when you make them work. Take your pulse again five minutes after you have stopped exercising, and it should be more or less back to normal.

TRY IT YOURSELF

The easiest place to find your pulse is on your wrist or on your neck. Use your fingers to take your pulse. Don't use your thumb to do this as it has a pulse too, so things can get very confusing!

Taking your pulse.

The Blood System

The blood system is the transport system of the body. The blood vessels are like different types of road: the largest arteries and veins are like motorways; then branching off them are smaller vessels which are like main roads, while the smallest vessels, known as capillaries, are like the local roads where traffic stops to make deliveries to shops. It's from the capillaries that substances like oxygen and glucose sugar move from the blood to other body cells.

Your biggest artery is called the aorta and it is about the same diameter as your thumb. It carries blood out of the left ventricle of the heart as it starts on its journey round the body. Other arteries branch off it at various points, taking supplies of nutrients and oxygen to different organs and muscles.

But what happens if you don't let blood bring supplies of nutrients and oxygen to your muscles when they're working? Try the activity on page 13 and find out!

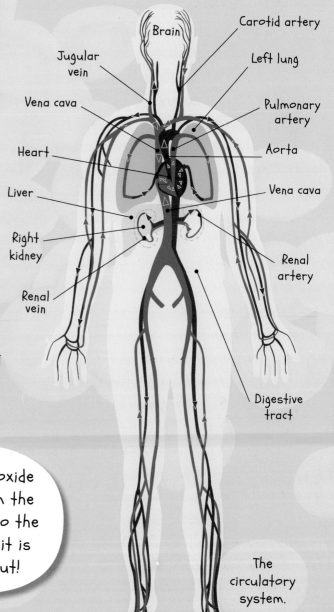

Brain

Carotid artery

Jugular vein

Left lung

Vena cava

Pulmonary artery

Heart

Aorta

Liver

Vena cava

Right kidney

Renal artery

Renal vein

Digestive tract

The circulatory system.

All carbon dioxide is taken from the vital organs to the lungs where it is breathed out!

Try it yourself

- Put one arm straight up in the air and let your other arm hang down by your side. Now clench and unclench both fists as hard as you can, about once every second.

- The hand that's up in the air will begin to hurt and your fingers will feel stiff.

- Stop clenching now and put down the arm that was in the air. In fact you have to, or your muscles will do it for you, because they'll get a cramp.

- So what just happened? Your muscles need oxygen and glucose sugar, which are carried by your blood, so that they can contract. They contract when you clench and unclench your hands.

- It's easy for blood to get to the muscles of the hand that's hanging down. But it's much harder for blood to get to the hand that's up in the air, because it has to flow against the pull of gravity.

- When your muscles don't get enough oxygen, a toxic substance called lactic acid builds up in them. This makes your muscles feel stiff and then cramp.

- When you put your arm down again blood can carry the lactic acid away to be broken down and the cramp stops.

Valves

One place where blood has to flow against gravity is from your feet and up your legs so it can get back to your heart. To help it along, the veins in your legs have valves in them to keep blood flowing in the right direction.

Cartwheel

Why don't my ankles fill up with blood?

Closed Valves   Opened Valves

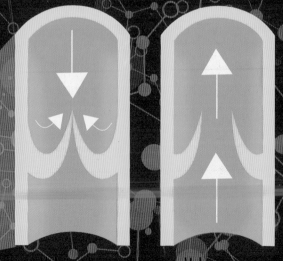

Valves close to stop blood flowing in the wrong direction, back down the leg.

Valves open to help the blood continue its flow in the right direction.

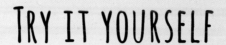

TRY IT YOURSELF

• If you clench your fist, you should see a pattern of bluish veins appear just under the skin on the back of your hand.

• With your finger, press down hard on an obvious vein near your wrist, and stroke it towards your knuckles. The blue colour should disappear from a section of the vein.

• When you take your finger away you should see it refill from the knuckle end. (This works best if your hands are warm.)

• What has happened is that you have massaged the blood out of a section of vein and by pressing on it, prevented it from refilling from the knuckle end of the vein. The one-way valves prevent it from refilling from the wrist end.

• Make sure you wait a few minutes before trying this again.

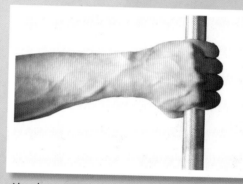

Hand veins.

In fact, all veins have valves in them. In your hands the veins are just under your skin, and you can see how the valves work.

The Gut

I bet you've never thought of yourself as a doughnut – but you really are like one: a very wonky, oddly shaped ring doughnut. Like a doughnut, you've got a hole that runs all the way through the middle of you, but it's much longer and wigglier than a doughnut hole.

This wiggly hole is your gut, and it goes all the way from your mouth at the top of your body, to your anus at the bottom (literally) – a distance of about ten metres.

The Gut.

Mouth

Oesophagus

Gall Bladder

Liver

Stomach

Pancreas

Duodenum

Small intestine

Large intestine

Appendix

Rectum

Anus

In a way the food you eat isn't really properly inside you while it's in your gut. It has to get out of your gut and into the rest of your body before it can do you any good.

Two key things happen in your gut:
- **Digestion** – Breaking food down into small, soluble molecules.
- **Absorption** – Moving these molecules through the gut wall and into the blood.

Digestion in the mouth

The digestion of food starts in your mouth.

• Get a cream cracker or a water biscuit. It doesn't matter which, as long as it doesn't have any sugar in it. Break it up into pieces, put it into your mouth and start chewing.

• Keep chewing!

• You need to keep the biscuit in your mouth for about two minutes. It's quite hard not to swallow it but try to resist!

• As time goes on, the mushy biscuit should start to taste sweet. This is because a chemical in your saliva has broken down the big molecules of starch in the biscuit into small molecules of sugar — which of course tastes sweet.

• You can swallow now, and you'll probably want a drink of water to wash all the mush off your teeth!

Digestion in the stomach

Digestion carries on in the stomach, which is a muscular bag. When it's empty it has a volume of about 50-70 millilitres. Normally it can stretch to hold about one litre (1000 millilitres), but it can be forced to stretch to hold about two to three litres, though that's very uncomfortable. Your stomach makes hydrochloric acid, which kills microbes on your food, and a chemical that breaks down protein.

No wonder it makes such funny noises!

Digestion in the small intestine

Digestion is completed in the small intestine. The food has now been broken down into molecules small enough to get out of the gut and to travel in the blood to the rest of the body. To make absorption of the molecules of digested food from the small intestine efficient, it needs a large surface area. It gets this by having millions of tiny projections called villi, which stick out into the river of digested food. Although each one is only two to three millimetres long, altogether they provide a huge surface area – about the same size as a tennis court!

Can you imagine how big?

By the time food gets to the end of the small intestine, all the useable nutrients have been absorbed. What is left is mainly fibre – bits of plant cells we can't digest – and water. Much of the water is removed in the large intestine, so by the time the waste gets to the end of the gut at the rectum and anus, it is semi-solid.

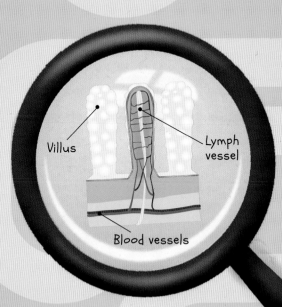

Villus

Lymph vessel

Blood vessels

Close up of villi.

The correct scientific name for it now is faeces, but you probably know it by other names!

The Lungs

The job of your lungs is to move air in and out of the body so that oxygen from inhaled air can pass into the blood to be carried to all your cells. It's equally important that carbon dioxide produced in your cells is taken in the blood to the lungs so your body can get rid of it. Breathing out is just as important as breathing in!

You breathe out to blow up a baloon or to blow bubbles.

Air breathed in:
79% nitrogen
20% oxygen
0.03% carbon dioxide

Air breathed out:
79% nitrogen
16% oxygen
3% carbon dioxide

The air you breathe in is made up of approximately 79% nitrogen, 20% oxygen and 0.03% carbon dioxide. You probably think that all of the oxygen is absorbed when it's in your lungs, but it's not. The air you breathe out is approximately 79% nitrogen, 16% oxygen and 3% carbon dioxide.

Exhaled air

This makes sense if you think about it – mouth-to-mouth resuscitation couldn't work unless there was a fairly high oxygen content in exhaled air. The carbon dioxide has increased in the air you breath out because it's a waste product of vital chemical reactions in your cells.

It's toxic, so you have to get rid of it quickly (in fact your body is more sensitive to changes in carbon dioxide levels than it is to changes in oxygen levels). When you hold your breath, it's the increased carbon dioxide that makes you stop, not the fact that your body is running out of oxygen.

The respiratory system.

Nasal cavity

Trachea

Bronchi

Breathing in and breathing out.

Lungs

To find out what is inside the lungs turn to the next page!

Diaphragm

21

What are your lungs like inside?

Pleural membrane

Bronchi

Bronchioles

Alveoli

The human lungs.

You might think that your lungs are like balloons, but in fact they're far more like sponges. Instead of one big space inside them, there are millions of tiny spaces. This is much more efficient for moving oxygen and carbon dioxide in and out of the blood. For this to happen, you don't just need plenty of space in the lungs, you need lots of blood vessels nearby. Having lots of tiny air sacs (called alveoli), each with blood capillaries in their walls, is much better for this than having one big space with one wall, because you can fit in far more blood vessels.

Breath holding

The average person can hold their breath for 30-40 seconds, but if you look up world records, you'll find people who can hold their breath for several minutes! Most of these records are set under water. This is because the body can react to being under cold water in ways that slow down oxygen consumption and carbon dioxide production, allowing the breath to be held for longer. This can be very dangerous so definitely do not try this yourself!

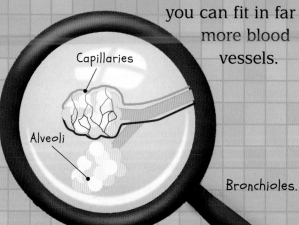

Capillaries

Alveoli

Bronchioles.

TRY IT YOURSELF

How much do your lungs hold? Ask an adult to help you with the following experiment.

You will need:

I measuring jug

I empty plastic bottle – at least two litres, three if possible

A waterproof marker pen

I piece of clean flexible plastic tubing (you can get this from aquarium supply shops, or maybe your school science department might lend you a piece)

1. Use the measuring jug to put 500 millilitres of water into the bottle.

2. Mark the water level on the side of the bottle with the pen.

3. Add another 500 millilitres and mark the new level.

4. Keep doing this until the bottle is full.

5. Put a few centimetres of water in a sink or bucket.

6. Put your hand over the top of the full bottle, turn it upside down, put the top of the bottle under the water in the sink or bucket and take your hand away. All the water should stay in the bottle!

7. Carefully, wiggle one end of the plastic tubing inside the bottle top.

8. Take a deep breath, put the other end of the tube in your mouth and blow as hard as you can! (Make sure you don't accidentally breathe in and swallow the water!)

9. The air you blow out pushes the same volume of water out of the bottle. You can read the scale you put on the bottle to find out the volume of air you were able to breathe out.

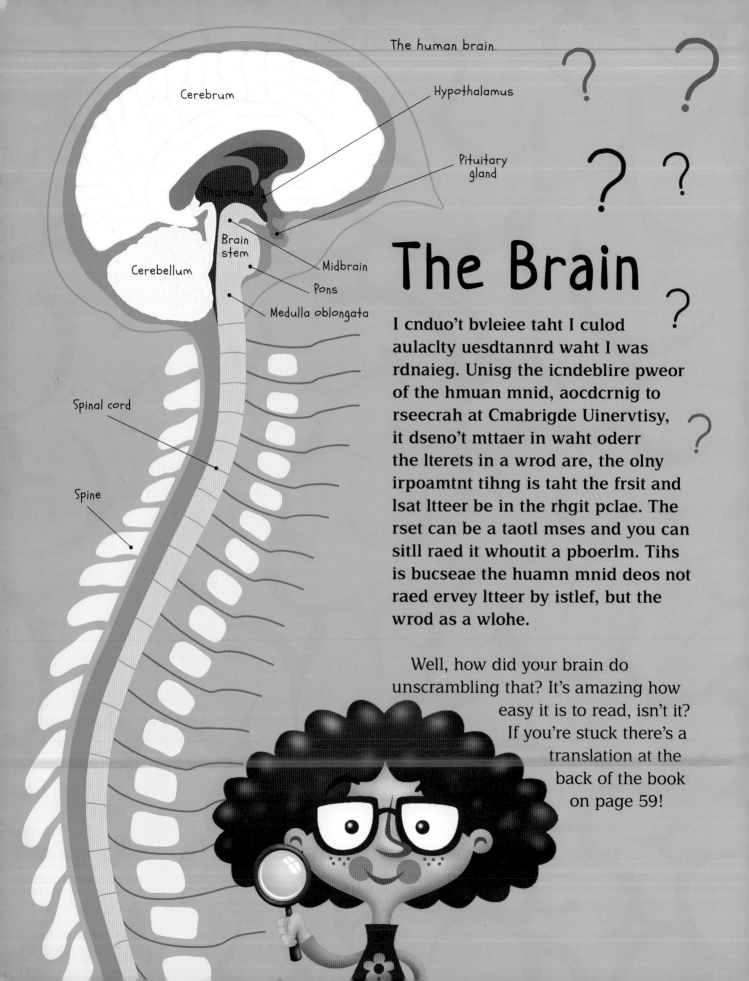

The human brain.

Cerebrum

Hypothalamus

Pituitary gland

Thalamus

Brain stem

Cerebellum

Midbrain

Pons

Medulla oblongata

Spinal cord

Spine

The Brain

I cnduo't bvleiee taht I culod aulaclty uesdtannrd waht I was rdnaieg. Unisg the icndeblire pweor of the hmuan mnid, aocdcrnig to rseecrah at Cmabrigde Uinervtisy, it dseno't mttaer in waht oderr the lteerts in a wrod are, the olny irpoamtnt tihng is taht the frsit and lsat ltteer be in the rhgit pclae. The rset can be a taotl mses and you can sitll raed it whoutit a pboerlm. Tihs is bucseae the huamn mnid deos not raed ervey ltteer by istlef, but the wrod as a wlohe.

Well, how did your brain do unscrambling that? It's amazing how easy it is to read, isn't it? If you're stuck there's a translation at the back of the book on page 59!

- The brain contains between 85 billion and 100 billion cells.

- The brain and spinal cord are a bit like a long, wrinkled sock. The 'foot' of the sock is folded back on itself to make the brain. The 'leg' of the sock is the spinal cord, which runs down the inside of the backbone. The brain and spinal cord are hollow, just like the sock, but unlike the sock (unless you're washing it) they are filled with and surrounded by fluid.

- Human brains are three times as big as those of other mammals the same size.

Bizarre brain facts

Of all the extraordinary organs of the body, the brain is the most amazing. Here are a few mind-boggling statistics.

- Each cell is connected to about 10,000 other brain cells.

- The brain has no pain receptors, so cannot feel pain.

- The brain makes up only about 2% of our bodyweight, but uses about 20% of the body's energy.

- The brain is protected by your skull, which is made of 22 bones.

- Your brain stops producing new cells when you are about 18. When the cells die, they aren't replaced.

- The right side of your brain controls the left side of your body and the left side of your brain controls the right side of your body!

Brain functions

Below is a basic diagram of the human brain and it's various functions.

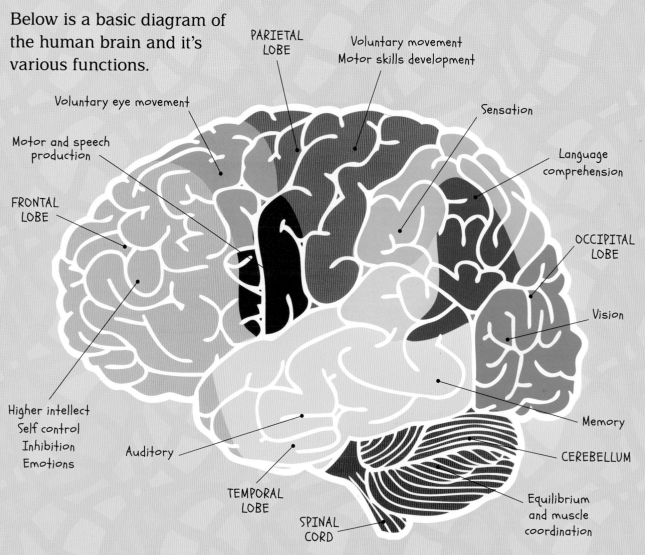

PARIETAL LOBE

Voluntary movement
Motor skills development

Sensation

Voluntary eye movement

Language comprehension

Motor and speech production

FRONTAL LOBE

OCCIPITAL LOBE

Vision

Higher intellect
Self control
Inhibition
Emotions

Auditory

Memory

CEREBELLUM

TEMPORAL LOBE

SPINAL CORD

Equilibrium and muscle coordination

Cerebral hemispheres

Different areas of the brain have different jobs. All the things that make you 'you' happen in the cerebral hemispheres. This is where signals from your sense organs are processed, and where the nerve impulses to your muscles start.
It's the area responsible for speech, personality and memory.

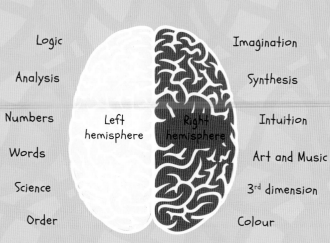

Logic

Analysis

Numbers

Words

Science

Order

Left hemisphere

Imagination

Synthesis

Intuition

Art and Music

3rd dimension

Colour

Right hemisphere

The jobs of each hemisphere of our brain.

Cerebellum

The cerebellum is where complicated movements are controlled. When you learn to do something like ride a bike or play a musical instrument, it's your cerebellum that 'learns' the sequence of movements. Once you have learned something, the information can be stored for years – once you learn to cycle, even if you don't get on a bike for years, you can still do it (though you may be a bit wobbly).

Optical illusions

The jumbled up passage at the beginning of this section shows how efficient the brain is at sorting out mixed up things, but you can fool it.

This is how optical illusions work. The brain will make a pattern out of the information it gets from the eyes if it possibly can, which is why these illusions work.

Medulla

The medulla keeps you breathing and keeps your heart beating. These are automatic functions, which is just as well. Imagine if you were eating your lunch and having a conversation, and you had to decide when to take each breath so you could keep doing both! Of course, you can deliberately change your breathing rate – but most people can't control their heart rate.

Do I breathe or do I eat?

The Nervous System

The nervous system brings information to your brain and spinal cord, and carries signals from them telling the rest of your body what to do. The fastest signals are called reflexes. These are very fast reactions to potentially damaging events that – hopefully – prevent the damage from taking place. To make them as fast as possible, reflexes don't even involve the brain: information goes to the spinal cord and straight back out again.

For instance, if you accidentally put your finger in a candle flame, you pull it out so quickly that it doesn't hurt until after you've taken it out. This is because pain sensors in your skin send a signal to your spinal cord, which sends another signal straight to the muscles of the hand and arm saying, get that finger out of there! Meanwhile, another signal goes to the brain, but it takes longer, because it has further to travel. This is the one that lets you know it hurts, but you've already removed your finger from danger. Definitely don't try this yourself as it will hurt!

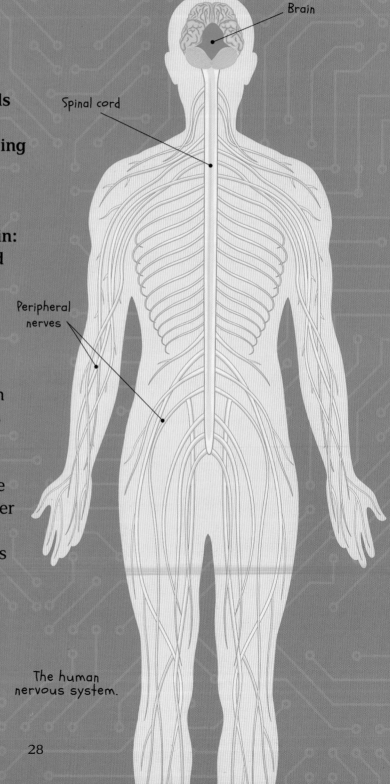

Brain

Spinal cord

Peripheral nerves

The human nervous system.

Reflexes

You have lots of reflexes: coughing, sneezing, knee-jerk, blinking and many more.

TRY IT YOURSELF

Here are two reflexes you can investigate safely. Turn to page 30 for the second experiment

1. You can find the knee-jerk reflex quite easily.

• Get a partner to sit with their legs crossed over each other so that the top leg swings freely and the foot doesn't touch the ground.

• Use your hand to feel for the lower edge of their knee cap, just below the knee.

• Use the side of your hand furthest from your thumb to hit just below the knee cap — not too hard!

• If you hit the right place, the lower leg will immediately kick out. Make sure you're not standing in the way when it does!

TRY IT YOURSELF

2. The pupil of your eye (the black bit in the middle of the iris), regulates how much light gets in and reaches the retina at the back of the eye. In bright light the pupil is quite small, as too much light can damage the retina, but in dim light it gets much bigger. There are two ways you can investigate this.

• Get a friend to close their eyes tightly for 30 seconds with their hands over their eyes to make it extra dark. Do this in a brightly lit room. When they open their eyes again, watch closely and you will see their pupils shrink — it happens quickly, so be ready!

• You can do this experiment by yourself too. Sit in front of a mirror in a brightly lit room. Shut and cover one eye as described above. Watch your eyes in the mirror as you open the closed eye, and you should see that the pupil of that eye is bigger than the one that was open, but quickly shrinks to the same size.

Pupils in bright light

Pupils in dim light

Reaction time

Reaction time is the time between seeing or hearing a signal, and starting to move in response to it. For most people, reaction time is about 0.25 seconds, but for top athletes, especially sprinters, it is faster – between 0.12 and 0.18 seconds. This can make all the difference to who wins a race like the 100 metres.

There is a limit to how fast you can react: it takes a certain minimum time for you to hear or see the start signal, for your brain to process that information and for it to send a message to your muscles to start moving. The shortest time this can take is 0.11 seconds.

If the athlete starts to move less than 0.11 seconds after the starting signal, their brain must have sent the signal to their muscles before the start signal, so even though they didn't move until after the signal, it's still a false start.

TRY IT YOURSELF

You can test your own reaction time with nothing more complicated than a 30 centimetre ruler — but you also need a friend to help you.

1. Get your friend to hold the ruler with the 0 centimetre end down.

2. Have your thumb and forefinger just either side of the 0 centimetre mark.

3. Ask your friend to let go of the ruler and see how fast you can catch it. Make a note of how many centimetres it falls.

4. Do this ten times. Add up your results and divide by ten to get an average time. There is a chart on page 58 that lets you convert this into a reaction time.

The Nose and Tongue

Your senses of smell and taste are very hard to separate. Quite a bit of what we think of as the taste of food is actually its smell. You might be aware of this if you've ever had a cold – if your nose is blocked, food seems to lose a lot of its taste.

Smell

Your nose is lined with special receptor cells which can detect about 1000 different types of chemical. Each chemical fits into a special area on the surface of one type of cell, like a key fitting into a lock, and when this happens, a signal is sent to the brain. The brain interprets this signal as a smell.

We have about 1000 different types of receptor cell, but scientists think we can identify up to 10,000 different smells. How can this work? The same way that the 26 letters of the alphabet can be used to make thousands of different words – by combining signals from different receptor cells when they get to the brain.

Some people have a much more sensitive sense of smell than others, and your sense of smell gets poorer as you get older. If you have a really good sense of smell, you could end up working as a 'nose', or perfumer. This is someone who develops perfumes and they need a really, really good sense of smell.

Here's a puzzle: no one really understands how we can remember smells. The cells in your nose die and are replaced all the time, but you don't forget what oranges or roses smell like.

One of the most expensive perfume scents Ambergris, is produced in the digestive system of a whale!

Perfume Recipe

TOP SECRET

TRY IT YOURSELF

Think about what you're smelling! Although we are very sensitive to smells, we often don't pay much attention to them (unless they're really delicious or really horrible). What does a tennis ball smell like? Or a leaf? Or this book?

Blindfold a friend and let them smell lots of different things (nothing too horrible though — you still want them to be your friend when you finish the experiment!).

Try using fruits, herbs and spices from the kitchen, soaps and lotions from the bathroom and, of course, perfume. How many can they identify?

Taste

Look at your tongue in the mirror. It's covered in lumps and bumps. It's OK, it's supposed to look like that! Those lumps are your taste buds. They contain receptor cells, similar to the ones in your nose, but they can't detect nearly as many different chemicals.

Try it yourself

Make a taste map of your tongue! You will need:

50 millilitres of water with 1/4 teaspoon of salt in it (salty)

50 millilitres of water with a teaspoon of sugar in it (sweet)

The juice of half a lemon (sour)

Tonic water (bitter)

Soy sauce (umami)

Cotton buds

1. Draw a large tongue shape on a sheet of paper.

2. Dip a cotton bud in the salty water. Dab it onto different areas of your tongue and make a note on your tongue diagram of where you can taste salt.

3. Repeat with a fresh cotton bud for each of the other liquids

4. Now you should have a map of which parts of your tongue are sensitive to which flavours. Check the one on page 35 to see if you agree with scientific theory!

In fact, there are only five different basic tastes! They are sweet, salt, sour, bitter and umami. (Umami is a Japanese word for a really savoury flavour, and it has only recently been discovered that it's a basic taste.)

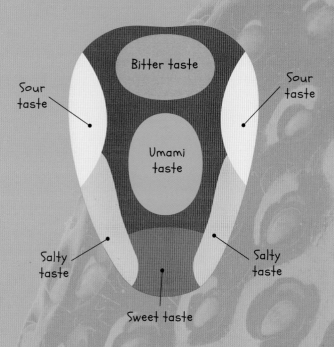

Bitter taste

Sour taste

Sour taste

Umami taste

Salty taste

Salty taste

Sweet taste

Tongue taste map.

Fooling your sense of taste

What you think of as your sense of taste is partly your sense of smell, but that's not all. Your sense of taste is also influenced by what your food looks like…

TRY IT YOURSELF

Ask an adult if you can carry out the following experiments to see how your sense of smell affects your taste…

1. Ask an adult to help you cut some small cubes of peeled apple, onion and carrot.

2. Blindfold a friend and get them to hold their nose tightly — make sure they remember to breathe through their mouth!

3. Get the blindfolded person to stick their tongue out, and put a cube of food on it. See if the other person can identify it just by taste without smell to help them — it's not as easy as you think!

To see how the colour of food affects your sense of taste, you need to make some jelly. You will need:

- Gelatine or the vegetarian equivalent
- Food colouring
- Flavouring essences

You need to make up the jelly according to the instructions on the gelatine packet, add flavouring, and then add the wrong colour. For instance, you could make strawberry flavoured jelly and then add green food colouring, or pink lemon jelly, or blue apple jelly! When it's set, see if other people can work out what the flavour is. Make up a few different combinations and have fun!

The Ear

Your ears allow you to hear (you already knew that!), but they also help to prevent you falling over. No, not because they're really big and stick out and act like the stabilisers on a bike. But because they are responsible for your sense of balance.

Hearing

Humans don't have particularly good hearing. If you have a dog, you'll know that they can hear sounds that are much quieter and higher pitched than us. You may also have noticed that, unlike humans, they can move their ears to help them detect sound.

Here's how your ear works to let you hear sounds. Sound waves hit the eardrum and make it vibrate. These vibrations are passed on to the hammer, anvil and stirrup (the three smallest bones in the body). As these bones vibrate, they amplify sounds by about 20 times. So what you think you hear is really 20 times quieter than it sounds! The vibrations are passed on through other parts of the ear until they reach the cochlea. Here, special cells change them into electrical signals, which travel along the auditory nerve to the brain.

Animals like dolphins and bats use ultrasound to communicate. These are sounds *above* the human hearing range, so we cannot hear them. Elephants and giraffes communicate using infrasounds. These are sounds *under* the human hearing range, so we cannot hear them very well.

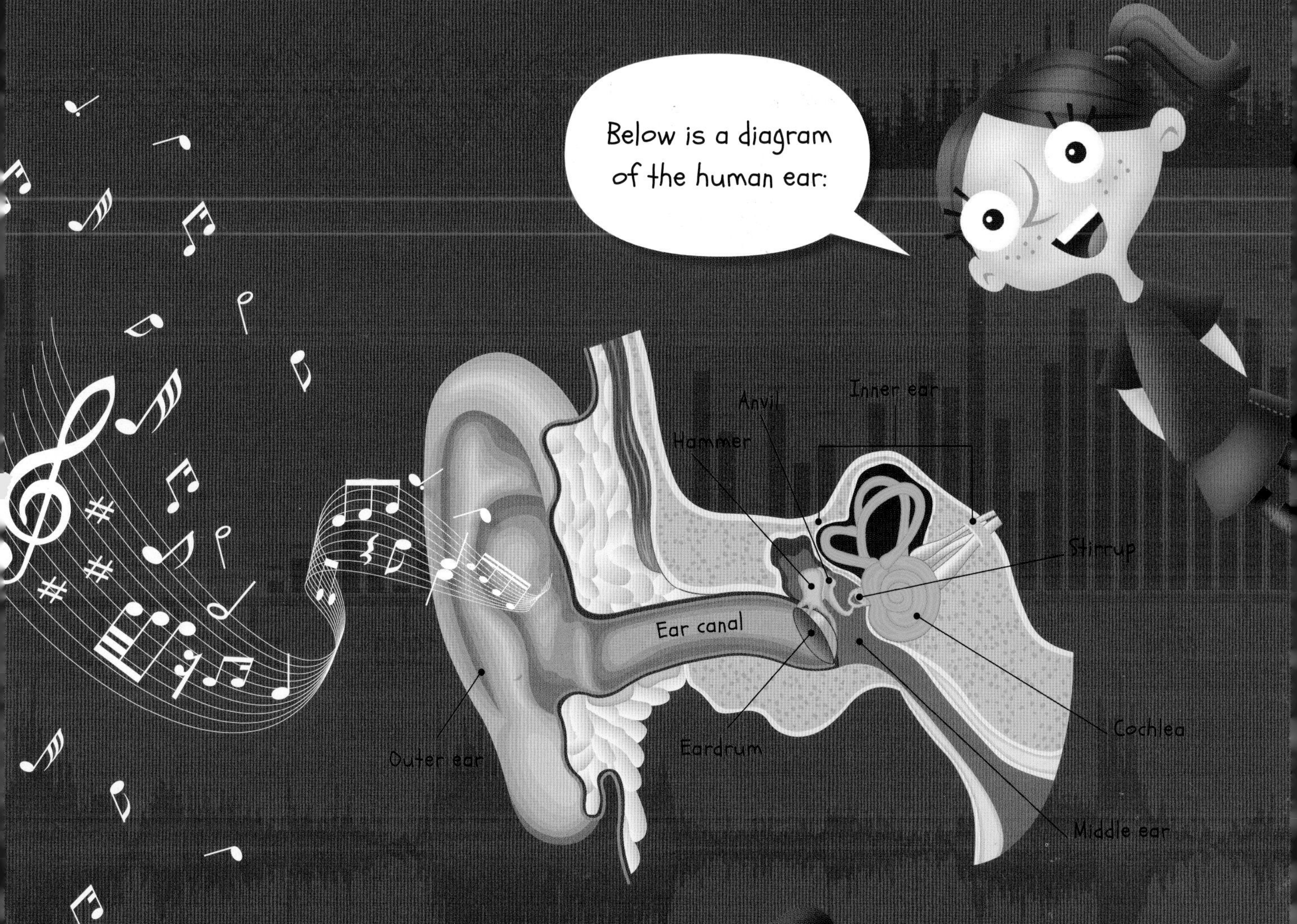
Below is a diagram of the human ear:
Anvil
Inner ear
Hammer
Stirrup
Ear canal
Cochlea
Outer ear
Eardrum
Middle ear

Age and hearing

As you get older, you get less able to hear very high-pitched sounds. Children can hear the ultrasonic sounds that bats make, but adults can't. There's a rather sneaky piece of modern technology called the Mosquito Anti-Loitering Device that makes use of this fact to stop children and teenagers hanging about where they shouldn't be. It makes a high-pitched buzz, which is really unpleasant if you can hear it.

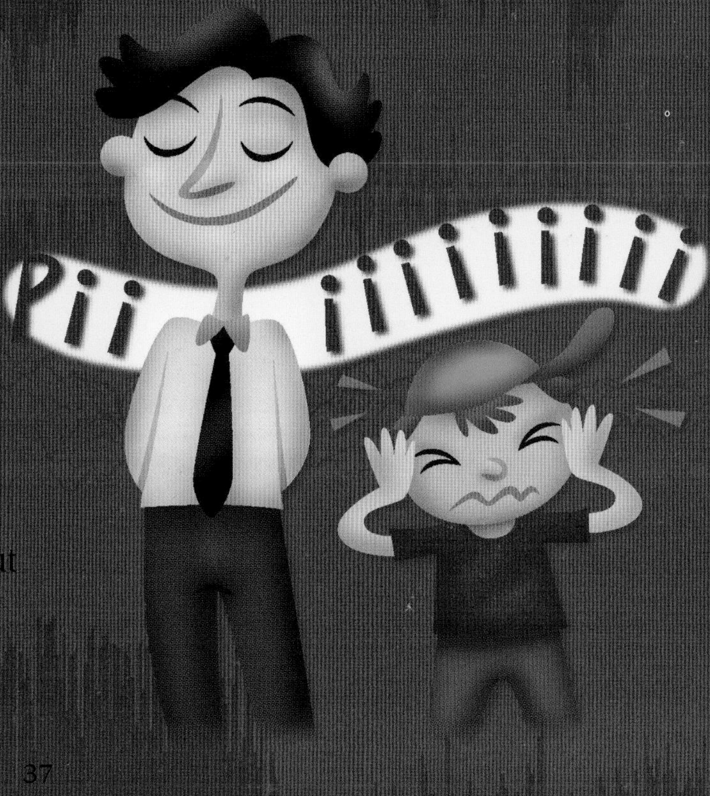
Piiiiiiiiiii

Balance

In the inner ear, buried deep inside your skull, are liquid-filled tubes that give you your sense of balance. They send messages about the position of your head to your brain. This will often save you from falling if you trip or lose your balance: the brain gets information that the position of your head has changed in an unexpected way and is able to make corrections fast enough for you to stay on your feet.

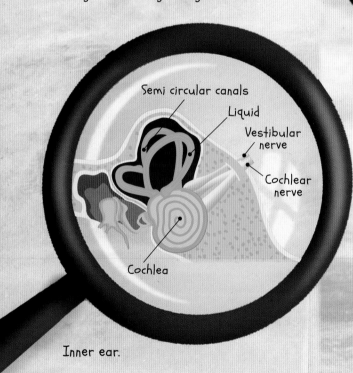

Semi circular canals

Liquid

Vestibular nerve

Cochlear nerve

Cochlea

Inner ear.

It's also the balance apparatus in your ears that makes you dizzy if you spin round and round. There are three semi-circular tubes (the semi-circular canals) at right angles to each other. They are filled with liquid.

You can find out about these simply by stirring a glass of water. The water goes round and round while you stir, and it keeps going round and round for a while even after you stop stirring.

This is what happens to the liquid in the semi-circular canals if you spin round and round. It starts moving as you spin, but when you stop, it keeps going. This means your ears are telling your brain that you're still moving, but your eyes are telling your brain that you have stopped. No wonder your brain gets confused!

Some people have to do a lot of spinning without getting dizzy and falling over, most notably ice skaters and ballet dancers. Do they have ears that are different from other people? No! They have a special trick called 'spotting' to avoid getting dizzy.

TRY IT YOURSELF

You're going to be spinning round, so make sure you do it somewhere safe so that if you fall over you won't hurt yourself or break anything else. And make sure you ask an adult before starting this experiment that it's ok to do so!

You already know that if you just spin round and round you'll get dizzy, so you don't need to try that bit. Instead, here's how to avoid getting dizzy.

• Look at something at about eye level. Maybe a picture on the wall, or a clock if you're indoors, a tree or a doorway if you are outside.

• Slowly turn your body, keeping your head still for as long as possible and still staring at the same spot.

• When you feel you can't turn your body any further without moving your head, turn your head round quickly (the same way as your body, obviously, or your head falls off — not really!) and stare at the same spot again.

• Once you get the hang of it, try the same technique when you spin round quickly. If you do this for every spin, you don't get dizzy, because your head only moves for a very short time, and the liquid in your semi-circular canals doesn't have enough time to start moving.

• If at any point you do start to feel dizzy, make sure you stop and sit down until you feel ok again.

The Eye

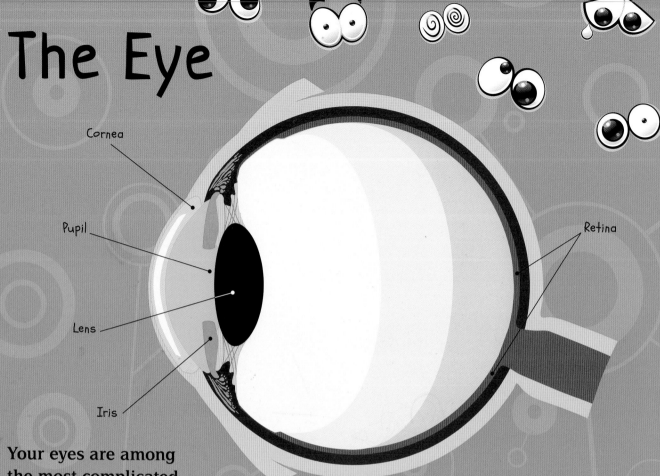

Cornea

Pupil

Lens

Iris

Retina

Your eyes are among the most complicated organs in the body. Here's a diagram of what one would look like cut down the middle.

Dilated pupil.

Letting light into the eye

The pupil and iris control how much light gets into the eye. The pupil is a hole in the centre of the iris – that's the coloured bit of your eye. The iris is a ring of muscle that can contract and relax to change the size of the pupil in the middle. In bright light, your pupils are quite small, but in dim light they get wider so as much light as possible can get into the eyes. If you go from bright light into a dark room, you can't see much at first. Your eyes gradually become 'dark adapted' as the pupils open wide. If you then go back into a bright light you have to screw your eyes up for a few seconds, because your wide pupils let in too much light.

Focussing

Your cornea and lens focus light so that a sharp image forms on the retina. If you are long or short-sighted however, it's a blurry image, unless you wear glasses or contact lenses.

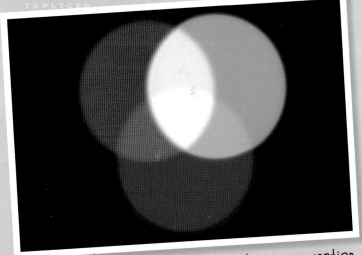

Additive primary colours, based on human perception of light.

How the retina works

The retina is covered with cells that detect light. They are called rods and cones. There are three types of cones, sensitive to red, blue and green light. These give you colour vision. They also give you a really detailed picture. When you look straight at something, you are pointing the area of the retina that has most cones at it. Rods only give you a picture in shades of grey, and in less detail than the cones, so you might think they're not nearly so useful – but they can work in much dimmer light than the cones. It's rods that let you see in dim light, or at night, and this is why you see everything in shades of grey at night.

TRY IT YOURSELF

On a clear, starry night, you can see the difference in how your rods and cones work. Look straight at a really dim star. Now look slightly to one side of it, and it will look brighter. This is because when you look straight at it you are pointing your cones, which are in the centre of the retina, at it and they don't work very well in dim light. When you look to one side you see it more clearly, because you are pointing your rods, which are round the edge of the retina, at it and they still work properly even in dim light.

Seeing the right way up!

The image that forms on your retina is upside down! It's your brain that turns it the right way up again. If you give someone special goggles that turn things upside down, the image on the retina is the right way up, but your brain still reverses it, so you see things upside down. However, your brain will adjust to what is going on after a couple of days, and turns things the right way up again. Of course, once you take the glasses off, everything is upside down again for a while...

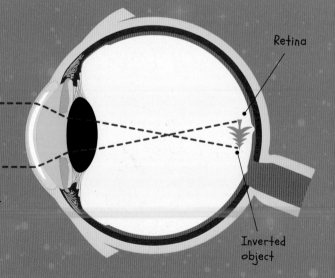

Retina

Object

Inverted object

TRY IT YOURSELF

You can demonstrate the upside down image by making a pinhole camera.

1. Take an empty potato crisp tube.

2. Get an adult to cut all the way round the can about five centimetres from the metal end.

3. Use a drawing pin to make a tiny hole in the centre of the metal end.

4. Fix a circle of tracing paper inside the plastic lid — this will be the screen where you see an image.

5. Put the lid on the short piece of tube, then fix the long bit on again with sticky tape.

6. Wrap a couple of layers of tinfoil round the whole thing, leaving the ends open, and fix it in place with sticky tape. This is to keep light out of the camera.

7. Take it outside on a sunny day and point it at something brightly lit — the object should appear upside down on the screen.

Why does this happen? It's because light travels in straight lines, so the light from the top of what you look at appears at the bottom of the screen.

(You can use a pinhole camera to take real photos if you get hold of some photographic film. See the back of the book for websites which will tell you how to do this.)

Pinhole camera.

Photo taken using a pinhole camera.

Blind spot

The light sensitive cells on your retina are attached to nerve cells that carry their messages to the brain. These all leave the retina at the same place, and there are no rods or cones on this bit of the retina. It is called the blind spot. You're not usually aware of its existence – there isn't a hole in the middle of what you see, even if you close one eye. But it's there all right…

TRY IT YOURSELF

You can demonstrate the blind spot using the diagram below.

● +

1. Hold the book up at arms length so the dot and cross are at eye level.

2. Close your right eye and look at the cross with your left eye.

3. Keep looking at it and very slowly bring the book towards you.

4. At some point, the dot will disappear! This is because its image is falling on your blind spot.

5. Repeat, this time closing your left eye and looking at the dot with your right eye.

But why don't you see a hole in the middle of things? Your brain fills it in, taking its cues from what you see around that area. It's usually so successful that you don't notice, unless you trick your brain like in this experiment.

Why do you see stars if you hit your head?

If you've ever given the back of your head a whack, you'll know that you 'see stars'. Maybe not quite like cartoon characters do, with birds flying round your head tweeting while the stars twinkle, but definitely flashing starry lights. The reason for this is that although your eyes are at the front of your head, the part of your brain responsible for vision, is right at the back of your head. If you hit it, your brain gets all sorts of weird signals, which it interprets as flashing lights and stars.

Definitely do not try this yourself.

The Skeletal System

An adult human has 206 bones. The largest is the femur, or thigh bone, and you've already met the smallest ones – the ear ossicles (that means 'tiny bones') or hammer, anvil and stirrup (see page 37).

Bone is hard and strong (although it's not the hardest substance in the body – that's the enamel on your teeth) and mainly made of a mineral called calcium phosphate. It's the calcium that makes bones hard; if you could remove the calcium, the bone would become bendy! Get an adult to help you with the experiment below to make some bendy bones!

TRY IT YOURSELF

1. Get a leg or wing bone from a chicken. It doesn't matter if it's cooked or not.

2. Put the bone in a jar and cover it with vinegar — any sort will do.

3. Put the lid on the jar tightly, then wash your hands carefully.

4. Leave it for at least three days.

5. After the three days, take out the bone and rinse it under cold water.

6. The vinegar should have dissolved away all the calcium in the bone, making the bone bendy. If it isn't bendy, put it back in the vinegar for another couple of days.

7. Wash your hands when you finish experimenting.

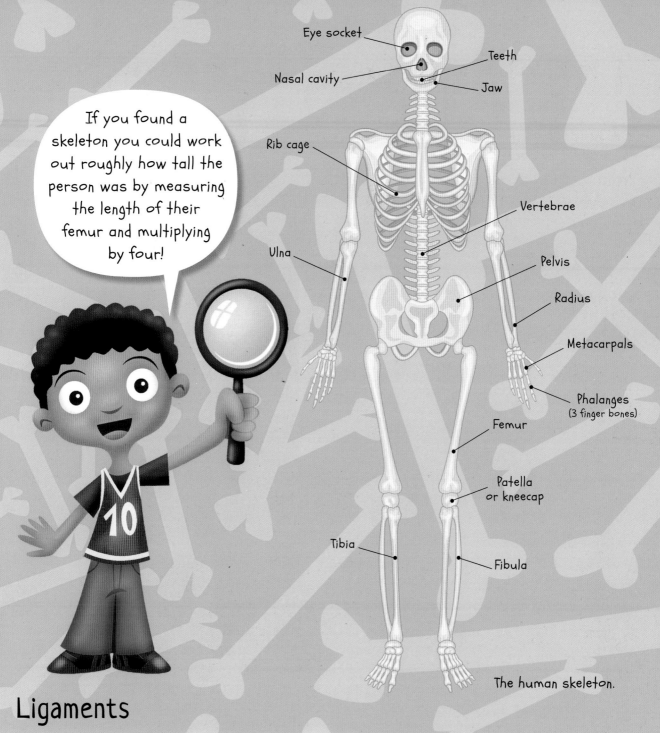

If you found a skeleton you could work out roughly how tall the person was by measuring the length of their femur and multiplying by four!

Eye socket

Nasal cavity

Teeth

Jaw

Rib cage

Vertebrae

Ulna

Pelvis

Radius

Metacarpals

Phalanges
(3 finger bones)

Femur

Patella
or kneecap

Tibia

Fibula

The human skeleton.

Ligaments

Bones are connected to each other by ligaments. These are made of tough, and slightly stretchy tissue (not the kind you blow your nose with!). Some people have extra-stretchy ligaments and can move their joints further than others. We sometimes call these people 'double-jointed', but they don't actually have double joints or twice as many joints.

The Muscle System

Muscles and bones work together to allow you to move. The bones form a system of levers and the muscles pull on them.

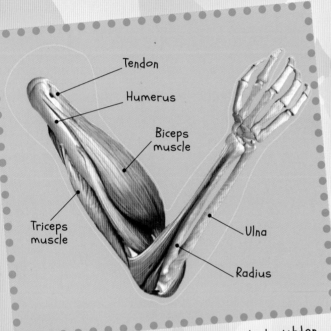

Muscles that pull on bones to bend and straighten your arm.

Labels: Tendon, Humerus, Biceps muscle, Triceps muscle, Ulna, Radius

All that spinach has made my muscles big and strong! But now none of my clothes fit!

The biceps and triceps produce opposite effects when they contract. When one contracts, the other relaxes. When the biceps contracts, the triceps relaxes and the arm bends at the elbow. When the triceps contracts the biceps relaxes and the arm straightens. If you bend your arm and tense your biceps you can see and feel it sticking up.

Muscles are connected to bones by tendons. It's important that tendons don't stretch, or when a muscle contracted it would stretch the tendon instead of pulling on the bone. Spinach is a great source of Iron and vitamins that helps your muscles to work better.

TRY IT YOURSELF

If you want to know more about muscles, tendons, bones and ligaments and how they fit together, you need to cut something up — but not yourself! Ask an adult to help you with the experiment below.

You will need:

A chicken wing

A small pair of sharp, pointed scissors and a small sharp knife

Some disposable gloves (but these aren't essential)

A magnifying glass

You will find the web address for instructions on what to do at the back of the book. Make sure you ask an adult's permission before you start your experiment and get them to help you do the cutting.

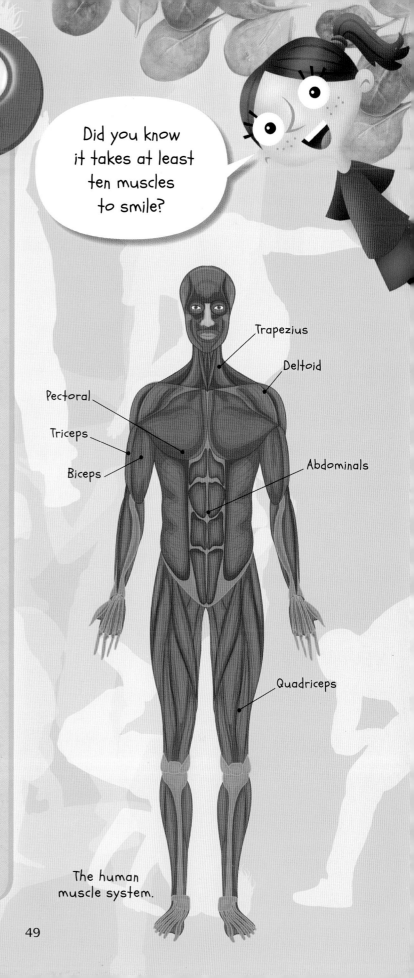

Did you know it takes at least ten muscles to smile?

Trapezius

Deltoid

Pectoral

Triceps

Biceps

Abdominals

Quadriceps

The human muscle system.

49

You can't try it yourself!

There are some systems in the body that you can't investigate by doing experiments at home. This doesn't mean they aren't important though!

Here's a quick tour round them.

The urinary system

If you eat more protein than you need, it gets broken down by the liver, because you can't store it in your body. One of the products of this breakdown is a toxic substance called urea, which your body needs to get rid of before it builds up.

This is your kidneys' job. They clean the blood, sending urea and other wastes to the bladder as urine. Each kidney contains over one million tiny filtering units. As well as removing urea, they ensure there are exactly the right concentrations of water and salts in the blood so that blood cells can work properly.

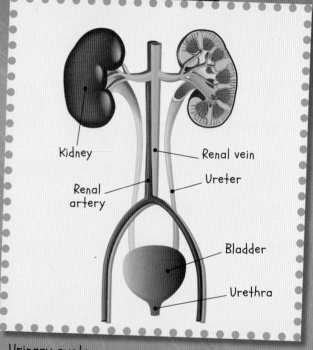

Kidney

Renal vein

Renal artery

Ureter

Bladder

Urethra

Urinary system.

The kidneys are like a washing machine for your blood!

You have two kidneys, each about the size of the palm of your hand. Every minute about one litre of blood passes through them to be filtered and cleaned.

The reproductive system

The job of the reproductive system is to produce special cells called gametes (sperm and eggs) and make sure they can meet. If they do and they join together, the resulting fertilised egg can develop into a baby.

The female reproductive system

In females, the two ovaries release eggs at a rate of about one per month. Each egg is about the size of a full stop. Before birth, a baby girl's ovaries already contain all the eggs she will ever release. The uterus provides a place where a fertilised egg can develop into a baby.

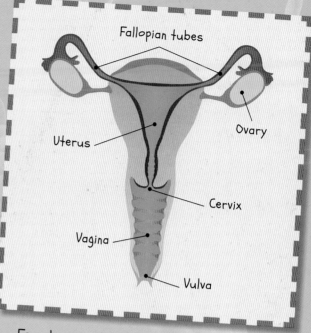

Female reproductive system.

Fertilised egg

Baby at 38 weeks (approximately 9 months)

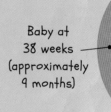

Elephants carry their babies for nearly two years!

Male reproductive system.

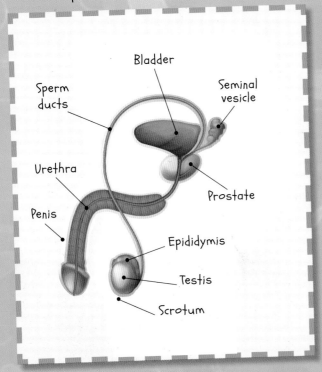

Bladder

Seminal vesicle

Sperm ducts

Urethra

Prostate

Penis

Epididymis

Testis

Scrotum

Sperm swimming towards the egg.

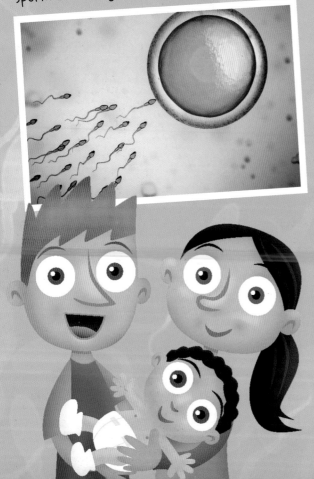

The male reproductive system

In adult males, the two testes produce sperm at the rate of 1000-1500 per second! Sperm are much smaller than eggs and, unlike eggs, they can swim (in fact, they look like tiny tadpoles). They are transferred into the female's reproductive system through the penis – then they have to swim for it. They all have to compete to get to the egg first, because only one can join with the egg to fertilise it. They only have about 17.5 centimetres to travel, but when you are only 0.05 millimetres long, that's a long way. It takes sperm anything from 45 minutes to three days to make the journey to the egg.

The lymphatic system

The lymphatic system is a sort of 'shadow twin' to the blood system. Like the blood system, it has vessels that run all through the body. It also has swellings called lymph nodes at various points. The lymphatic system has three different jobs:

1. It absorbs digested fats from the small intestine.

2. It mops up fluid that escapes from the blood capillaries and returns it to the blood system.

3. The lymph nodes contain lots of lymphocytes and act as a sort of 'security check' on blood passing through them. This is where antibodies and antigens get a chance to meet.

If you have an infection, you may find that you have swellings in your neck, armpits or groin. This is lymph nodes swelling because extra immune system cells are made here.

The hormone system

Hormones are chemicals that allow different parts of the body to communicate with each other. They are produced by glands in several areas of the body, and travel all round the body in the blood. Some hormones affect lots of other organs. Adrenalin, which you make if you get a fright, makes your heart beat faster, your pupils get wider, and your blood pressure increase. It diverts blood from the gut to the muscles, and suppresses your sense of pain and your need to pee. All these things help prepare you for an emergency where you might have to fight or run away.

Scary or exciting activities like going on a roller coaster make us produce adrenalin too.

Other hormones only affect one organ. For instance, antidiuretic hormone is produced in the brain but only affects the tiny filtering units in the kidney. It makes sure they keep the right amount of water in the blood and send the right amount to be lost in urine.

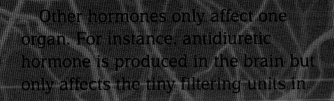

Girls produce some hormones in the ovaries, and boys produce the equivalent ones in the testis.

Male hormonal system.

Pituitary gland

Thyroid gland

Thymus

Adrenal glands

Pancreas

Testis

Female hormonal system.

Ovaries

The immune system

The immune system defends the body from foreign organisms like bacteria and viruses. The two types of white blood cell in the immune system do this in different ways.

Below is how Phagocytosis works...

Phagocytes

One type of white blood cell, called phagocytes, creeps up on foreign cells, gobbles them up and breaks them down. Although phagocytes are blood cells, they crawl out of the blood vessels and roam all over the body, looking for invading cells. If you have a spot, or an infected cut, you might see yellowish pus there. This is actually the bodies of brave phagocytes that have eaten themselves to death on bacteria as they defend you from disease.

1. Phagocyte meets bacterium.

Bacterium

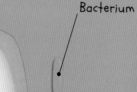

Nucleus

Phagocyte

2. Phagocyte engulfs bacterium.

3. Bacterium is destroyed by chemicals produced by phagocyte.

Bacterium broken down by chemicals

Lymphocytes

The other type – lymphocytes – stay in the blood. They produce specially shaped proteins called antibodies, which fit perfectly onto molecules called antigens on the surface of foreign cells. The antibody and antigen fit together like a lock and key. The antibodies help destroy the foreign cells, but this can take a few days, so you might be ill for a while before they are destroyed: this is what happens when you first meet the chickenpox virus, for instance.

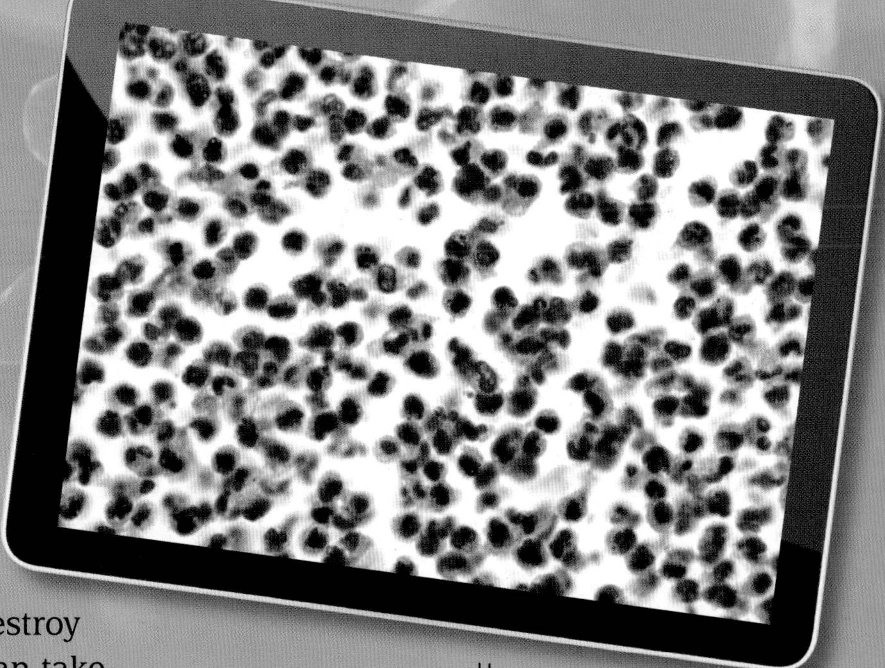

Human white blood cells.

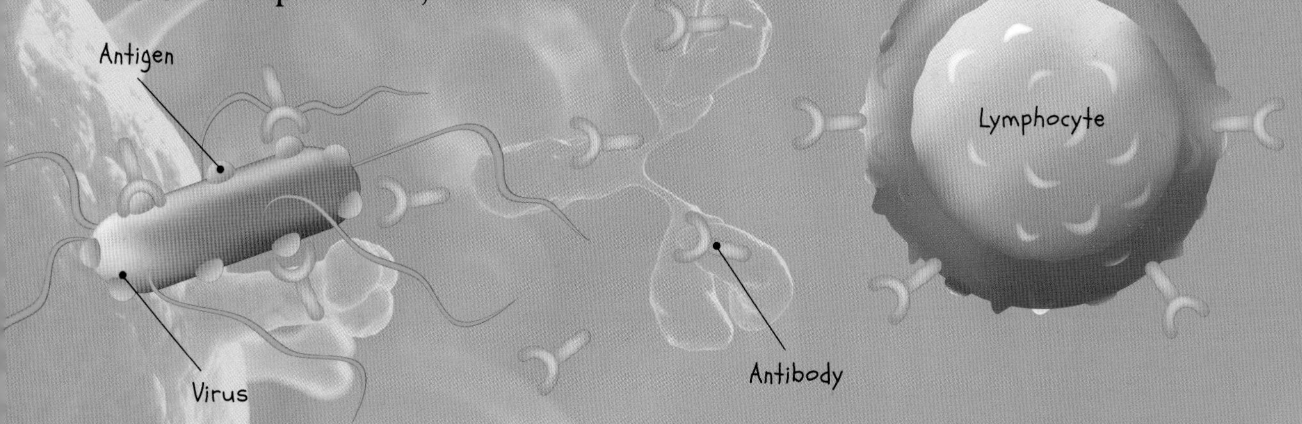

Antigen

Virus

Antibody

Lymphocyte

...And above is how antibodies defend you from intruders.

Some of the lymphocytes 'remember' meeting the virus, and if they come across it again, they produce antibodies so fast that you don't get ill. You are now immune to chickenpox, and won't catch it again.

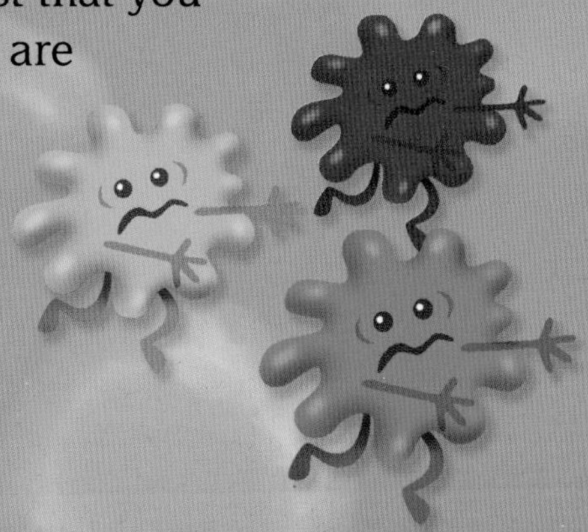

Centimetres fallen	Reaction time (s)
0	0.00
1	0.04
2	0.06
3	0.08
4	0.09
5	0.10
6	0.11
7	0.12
8	0.13
9	0.14
10	0.14
11	0.15
12	0.16
13	0.16
14	0.17
15	0.18
16	0.18
17	0.19
18	0.19
19	0.20
20	0.20
21	0.21
22	0.21
23	0.21
24	0.22
25	0.23
26	0.23
27	0.23
28	0.24
29	0.24
30	0.25

Here is the chart to find out your reaction time in seconds, as mentioned on page 31.

Experiments

For instructions on how to dissect a chicken wing (as mentioned on page 49) visit the address below. Remember to ask an adult before you do this.

www.biologyalive.com/life/classes/anatandphys/documents/Unit%206/ChickenWingDissection.pdf

Visit this address for instruction on how to make a pinhole camera that will take a photograph.

http://www.matchboxpinhole.com/index.html

Find Google images for 'Magic Eye Illusions' and be amazed!

For the translation to the scrambled paragraph of text on page 24 see below:

I couldn't believe that I could actually understand what I was reading. Using the incredible power of the human mind, according to research at Cambridge University, it doesn't matter in what order the letters in a word are, the only important thing is that the first and last letter are in the right place. The rest can be a total mess and you can still read it without a problem. This is because the human mind does not read every letter by itself, but the word as a whole.

Find out more

Read

Blame My Brain by Nicola Morgan (Walker, 2013)

Bloomsbury Discovery: My Body (Bloomsbury, 2014)

What Makes You YOU? by Gill Arbuthnott (Bloomsbury, 2013)

Watch

Fantastic Voyage (20th Century Fox, 1966)

Scientists in a special submarine shrink to the size of a human cell and are injected into the blood stream. Silly but fun!

Visit

The Camera Obscura in Edinburgh for all sorts of optical illusions, holograms and a giant pinhole camera.

http://www.camera-obscura.co.uk

The Science Museum in London.

http://www.sciencemuseum.org.uk

Log on to

Try some of the human body and mind games at the link below.

www.bbc.co.uk/science/humanbody

There are lots of reaction time tests you can find on the Internet.

One of the most fun ones to try involves shooting virtual sheep with tranquilliser darts! Visit the link below and have a go!

www.bbc.co.uk/humanbody/sleep/sheep

Glossary

Absorption Food molecules being moved through the gut wall into the blood

Adrenalin A hormone that is produced by the body in stressful situations

Alveoli Tiny air sacs in the lungs that help to move oxygen and carbon dioxide in and out of the blood

Antibodies Proteins that fight off disease by helping to destroy bacteria or virus cells

Antigens Molecules on the surface of foreign cells that cause the immune system to produce antibodies against them

Aorta The biggest artery in the human body, carrying blood from the heart

Arteries Blood vessels that carry blood containing oxygen and nutrients from the heart around the body

Auditory Relating to the sense of hearing

Blind spot The part of the retina that contains no rods or cones, so does not produce an image for you to see

Calcium A mineral contained in bone that makes it hard

Capillaries The smallest blood vessels. They let oxygen and nutrients move from the blood to other body cells

Cells Small units that are the 'building blocks' of the body

Cerebellum The part of your brain where complicated movements are controlled

Cerebral hemispheres The two halves of your brain. Each hemisphere has different jobs

Consumption Taking in

Contract Shortening of a muscle, making it tense up

Cramp A sharp pain in your muscles caused by lack of oxygen

Dermis The deeper layer of skin underneath the epidermis

Dissecting Cutting something up in order to study it

Diuretic Something that encourages the production of urine

Enamel The hardest substance in the body, which teeth are made of

Epidermis The outer layer of the skin, which is constantly replaced

Femur Thigh bone, the largest bone in the human body

Gametes Sperm and egg cells

Glands Organs that store chemicals for use in the body

Glucose A type of sugar that comes from carbohydrate foods

Hormones Chemicals that allow different parts of the body to communicate with each other

Humid A high level of water in the atmosphere

Immune Resistant to an infection or disease

Ligaments Slightly stretchy tissue that connects different bones to each other, forming joints

Lymph Liquid that circulates through the lymphatic system

Lymphocytes White blood cells that fight off disease by making antibodies to kill bacteria or virus cells

Medulla The part of your brain that keeps the automatic body functions going (breathing and heartbeat)

Microbes Tiny organisms made of a single cell

Mouth-to-mouth resuscitation Breathing into someone else's mouth to help them start breathing again if they have stopped

Nutrients Substances that provide what the body needs to grow and survive

Optical illusion Images that trick the brain into seeing something different from what is really there

Organs Collections of tissues that form a body part with a specific function

Phagocytes White blood cells that fight off disease by breaking down bacteria or virus cells

Pus A fluid formed in infected tissue

Reaction time The time between seeing or hearing a signal, and starting to move in response to it

Receptor cells Cells that receive chemical signals from elsewhere in the body

Reflexes Very fast reactions to potentially damaging events, which go straight to and from the spinal cord without involving the brain

Relax Lengthening of a muscle, reducing tension

Retina The part of the eye that detects light and on which an image forms

Sprinters Athletes who run extremely fast for short distances

Starch A carbohydrate made from glucose

Tendons Tissues that connect muscles to bones

Toxic Poisonous

Ultrasound High-pitched sounds that are above the human hearing range so can't be heard by humans

Umami A really savoury flavour

Urea A toxic substance formed from the breakdown of protein. It is cleaned from the blood by the kidney

Veins Blood vessels that carry blood from around the body back to the heart

Villi Small finger-like projections that absorb nutrients from food as it passes through the small intestine

Virus A small infectious particle that reproduces itself inside the cells of living creatures

Index

Index